Crying in the Cheap Seats

Crying in the

Bill Tremblay

Cheap Seats

University of Massachusetts Press

To my wife, Cynthia

Contents

There is Only One Endless Poem

THERE is only one   endless   poem.

In the endless poem
there is a house   reared
in ecstasy   whose walls are

white screens where the ceaseless arc-lamp
projects through the sockets of my eyes
the energies between blood and galaxies

whose light reaches my chorded heart
strikes sparks from my bones
moves me, makes me   not   therefore I
but   sometimes always spread burning
along these three-tongued flames
intersection   and I am electrocuted.

I lay beside my brother   a while
he sleeps   I see
into the black rooms
a Canadian trapper,   a Norman
a mercenary Gaul for Rome   I am sick,
I know not why, I said to the dark lady:
It is guilt, she replied
you killed your own people for gold and salt.

And beyond him
a man waiting in a cave for dawn.

I was from the beginning
will and ever shall be   world
without end   Amen

WHEN I wake   trembling and reach
my lungs   my throat   catches
at the moving images   with the child
left behind the is breath makes

a new language of a June hill morning
the blue through elm green
welcome   that month my birth that blue
I am that   still

one with that   sky
and hill

THERE is a woman
the fall of her

long brown hair

we will be together in eternity
she says into the hollows of my hands

it returns   it returns
as an episode of whispering in the endless poem
the smooth curves of her

white naked body
curved above my tomb.

I am walking in the dark alleyway
(why is it always   the same   dark   alleyway?)
with Hegel   discussing the mind and heart

just as he is saying "you must have both"
we see a crowd
queued up before a theatre

a girl is drunk
is it   because she believes she loves
this man   she hates   cannot
stand sober knowing
                              yelling twisting
from his hands they hold her wrists

"Let her go," I tell him
softly, "you can't . . ."

"Mind your own business!"
he says   and I see in the pulsing lights
of the marquee
he is me

that summer   in Newport
she ran   I
hurt her wrists
to some stranger
her feet   were cut on the broken glass
who said   "Let her go."

Thus it is with the endless poem
:the people become other   other
the places   change.

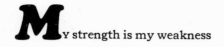**M**y strength is my weakness

if a heart could be bent back
into rightness
like a twisted horse-shoe

if I could make a ring with
the arms of the endless poem
in which to hold
a shattered grecian urn
together

the muscles
are nothing to the furious no!
of her   world   I broke

getting her to love me
then shoving my cock up her ass
till she screamed
why do you want to hurt me?

ICE diamonds over
every surface
                        the veins of trees
throb liquid sugars
through lucent maple barks
                                        life
hums swirling
radium grass waves sargasso
earthworms screw sod
building of organic fire bricks
  thinking motion

lovers in grassy commons the stillness

I see this as boy and man
it flows into me   the sign for promise it is
what I love with

My town is called Southbridge
its streets and gutters
run with the rain
of my memory

every space in it definite enough
to be a place
has an episode of the poem
hidden like a demigod in it.

I make my Via Dolorosa
through the cobbling streets of this town
how it flowed into me
how the outside world like the Quinebaug River
flooded my town of ecstasy
away.

I was born and was blinded
the silver nitrate (I dream of Chile
Andean mines) something went wrong

in dreams the surface of my body
passes through my mother's cervix
like hot pentothal waves
hearing across airwaves the radio chorusing
the machinery of muscle
drilling on the quadrangles of Nuremberg

the white high whir of truck tires
down the two-lane highways of the eastern seaboard
my father smelling of motor oil
and checklists

my mother after six black months
admitted I was blind
sitting on an oak bench worried over
the advent of a second hurt child
my brother's lungs ringing up one dime
closer to death with every cough

a definite time and place
I see for all
the doctor's sleight-of-hand

a celebration
the light of song painted on the eve
of Dionysus' murder   comets   roman candles   green

it was a warm night.

GOING to California   where I fly
above the bones of conquistadors
every fish in the Snake River winks at me
as I pass the continental divide

into the endless returning pictures

my family drives to Revere Beach   it is cold
I step with my aunt into the razored waters
reaching from a rock   struggling away
I plunge under   until they ran for help
and I rise dripping with the element

that very day
Mahatma Gandhi led thousands to the shore
there   they boiled seawater for salt to make them free

I saw their lean brown bodies tell
the world
let smoke rise into air from fire burning
water into earth:
one turn and the divide is crossed.

Boys and girls in a circle
around the grave of a cat

an altar boy in his black cassock
saying Our Father quick in Latin

they all go home to supper
he digs up the shoebox casket
of the cat he killed by throwing it
in the trash-barrel fire

puts the body on the tracks
where the 5:30 local
squishes it to fur   pulp   blood

what does he see
crouching over it
poking the guts with a stick?

They tell his mother
and she takes his hand and
burns it on the stove

how do you like it
she asks.

THE court we live on is a dead end:
a cyclone fence
and then the light and power company

a hundredfoot smokestack
coal burns   the sky is grey sometimes:
all night the transformers hum like locusts
to the sleepless

sitting on the steps I can see them all
the mothers   leaning out over railings
hanging clothes on spiderweb lines
from second-storey porches   in housecoats

battling against the soot
screaming across the street "Chris d'Calvie!"
when one kid gets beaten up by another

they wash and cook
and love their husbands one night
throw them out the next, sometimes saying
how they've been to confession to take
communion and no making love
hulking husbands stinking beer

and as if the Church were not enough
they go to a woman's house on Worcester Street
who drops two drops of olive oil   on water
and if they join it is the reason   the evil eye

a lot of them work the second shift
at the American Optical
I see them cutting down the sad path through
      the coal yard
and theirs is the death of cancerous mothers
and retarded children to be sent away to Belchertown

13

but mostly   it is   this picture
a mother shaking out a rug
on the back porch on a blue May morning
the month of Mary

she sings some simple song.

I stood in the soft tar
hot summer afternoon road
my breathing burning
my eyes blurred and saw faintly red
shimmering like Utah

I prayed to the Devil
to send her   the one who would
go with me   into the pine world

we would tear off our clothes
and ravage each other
crying in the sudden stab of orgasm
when it came.

Against that choice
the faces of Jesus, Mary, and Joseph
could weep marble tears
forever.

STRANDS of people's lives begin to
braid in the poem.

The mean kid stoned the skinny kid
on the crown of his skull   the blood
was fire in the forest of his hair
it streamed as he ran to his mother
crying through the weeds and burr.

The mean kid years later
stood at night with me in the coal yards
asking me to please teach him
words   And it was a clear starry
night and I said the word for that
was "obituary."

The skinny kid is sitting on the veranda
of the country club   collapsed
draped in a blanket   soaking wet   crying
begging   saying
"I couldn't save him, he was too big,
he would have . . . I tried!"
his dark hair wet with another blood
his big idiot friend I saw   his body
delicate as beached jellyfish
his face puffed up   his mother
old in her thirties the mother of thirteen
children and a drinking husband   stared at it
her arms crossed under her breasts   her breasts
only covered with a threadbare sweater
smelling the smell of fish as if
dying there had made him   aquatic
weeds and the mud at the bottom of ponds
reeking from his grapplehook-punctured body
and said   "Good enough for him."

TREE top high at the powerline clearing
the hawk swayed
staring off east toward the cool ponds
when the flick of lead through leaves
sent him spinning into the sun

a pack of bluejays mobbed him
tearing at him with their beaks
until he circled back   exhausted

the hawk clutched the branches
with his talons, his eyes
sharp   his breast burning

and when he was hit
he spiralled down
and   still he was alive
screaming and fluttering in the laurel
until his head was bashed in with a gunbutt

and even when he was nailed
to the garage door
there was   still   that fire.

OUR hero would get drunk
and howl out car windows
down long back roads in Connecticut
his hand clenching a quart of beer
his other the steering wheel
of a '36 Ford going 70, 80, 90 miles an hour

it was drinking after school
and all weekends with blowjobs from this
guy in a beret
and screwing chicks as crazy as him
and fights   legit like football
or streetfights   barfights
screamfits in drugstores

and gratuitous terror
lifting a 200-pound boulder over his head
crashing it through the hood of a parker's car
the rest of us   rocking the car
the girl   screaming   the guy
locking his doors

THE advantage of Elm Street:
memories triple up
people dispose themselves in time

I leap Olympian from screen to screen
Southbridge poems jangle in my head
the catalog of merchandise on Elm Street

the fruits watermelon cantaloupe and cool
green seedless grapes in wooden boxes
in the street beside the cash 'n carry Colonade
wagons in a row bicycles   the mean kid and I
steal one one Thursday shopping night
my momma   she pulled my pants down
and slapped my ass red for that one

I can hardly see straight
the Moroccan plunder of it all   the words.

Or in the Strand Theatre on Elm Street
all the world   Hollywood version   flickers
before me   Trader Horn in Africa   and
there were pretty tough chicks who wore butch cuts
and sat in the show with you on Saturdays

they wore wranglers   and nylon jackets
with no bras
you pulled their tits
they jerked you off while chewing bubble gum

watching the impalas the cheetahs the giraffe's
fifteen-foot stride   I am the antelope
this lioness licks my loin
I can't stop looking at the superimposition.

I hear the sound of voices laughing
in the grasses beyond the sandbanks
it is two girls and a boy   I know them   on the stage
the sun makes in clearings, the trees
curtains
            naked they burn
a jet of their Panic vapors enters me

a month later these same and more have almost
an orgy

three years later in this location
Oak Hill Cemetery
the girl I took into the laurel with me
to make a secret with   is drunk on muscatel
with me and two other guys
she goes down with one
the other guy says "Let's watch them"

I walk away
shaking my head : I
became a criminal for her?

I see these woods between the neighborhoods
and graveyards in time
                            spring, and leaves bud, ripen
fall, snow in hard slants
every color dark japanese print winter
under pines single sumac fragile sticks ink
the oak is sleeping.

IN St. Mary's Church
the ceiling is heaven
and lithe angels in flowing white robes
never quite smile.

On Friday afternoons in Lent
old   Italian ladies in black
dresses, black shoes, balance on their knees
making the stations of the Cross

genuflecting before the fiery pictures
their faces wrinkled with pain
like fingernails torn to blood
of the only Christ for them.

My endless poem began with that
every afternoon I go to pray that God
will grant me a wonder singing

but I have this vision : a high church
like a cliff   wind grey howling
from the mouth of a clouded sky
old people dumping the trash of their dreams
into that void   it is God

I would walk outside   everything astonishing
the ice on Hamilton Street
the houses the railroad tracks Quinebaug River
woods   the high clay banks of Paige Hill
like the forehead of an Indian chief
the still early March sky above the stoic trees

everything sings its offering
oratorio's penetrating the agnostic skies
my eyes could rise to the black above the sun.

AFTER school I spend my time
down by the Quinebaug River

down past the coalyards
the river runs hard
in lists between huge concrete blocks

they were going to erect
a trestle for the Grand Trunk Railroad
on those blocks

"They died on the Titanic, those people
that owned that railroad," my mother said.

I hear the steamwhistle over the North Atlantic
busted bulkheads   the iceberg horn
panic and song   the ark of lights goes dark under

and so they left these concrete things
unfinished, the paws of sphinxes.

These human associations
this residence in the earth
mix flesh with the wood and stone of
our habitations

the thin fingers of a sampan woman
I see her cooking beans on an open fire
moored along a Chinese river

she knows the endless motion has worn it
thin on the stone mortar
grinding grain

she knows the grinding motion
of sex   the endless summer
of the tropic

just as the hawk knows the poem of flight
his eyes blaze with a man pleasure
his wings outstretched over a global updraft
the lady wind swirling
to make a hollow into the nest of the earth

the Quinebaug the North Atlantic the Yangtze
endless flowing flowing through now.

Machines & Tears

Duerme, no queda nada,
Una danza de muror agita las praderas
y America se amego de maquinas y llanto.
   —FEDERICO GARCIA LORCA
   "Ode to Walt Whitman"

I run my finger down the map
tracing the Quinebaug River's blue-veined course
how it merges with the Thames
and flows into Long Island Sound
and in old pictures I see packet boats
sailing to New York City

I am working for the American Optical
so I can go to college in New York City

the hurricane swelled the Quinebaug
breaking her dams   picking up three-deckers
in the Flats   these lumber stacks
floating them away till the ribs of wood
cracked at the dynamo turbine
the water rushing to the sea

my job is to scrape the disaster off
picking up 12-foot unplaned old pine boards
hurling them through July
seeing sweat my arms   my chest   an earth
with rivers each aching muscle

the master of the lumberyard
called Popeye, Pacific marine, his eyes Hawaii
his tattooed arms made flowered wahinnies hula
doing the work of three men
he leaped from the ground to the cab of his truck
loving the wood, stacking it, planing it

I could admire him   stay and be like him
strong bold a lover satisfied
a drinker a good man of Southbridge

but the river runs by where I work
calling and calling.

AUGUST afternoons
hover like purple flying needles
I break from work finding shade heaven
smoke a cigarette and read a book on Africa

mau-maus scream murder vows
in blood rituals I drink the earth mixed in
at night I dance drunk uhuru Kenyatta battlechants
singing Free dom!
vowing never to work 40 years
for a gold watch and a good screwing.

There's a world out there:
I   stretched out on the hot tongue of the sun.

THAT first day in New York City
standing on the upper deck of the Day Line
unsure the Hudson under the excursion
footing unsteady by brackish wakes

once around the magic isle
south into the bay   the green Lady
holding the torch toward the Brooklyn Bridge
its gothic spires slicing the air

where was Whitman? I wondered
where the Brooklyn ferry crossed the East

down the boat chugging like a sidewheeler
making the last arc
presenting the outside   the monument
buildings from the river distance their people
silent waiting sculptures
north american mute hieroglyphic
the red carnations of their lives in windowbox gardens.

THAT first night in Times Square
Christ the air is fumes from Satanic flesh pots
I am dying of TB
sharing the fate of my grandfather

romancing Broadway
I am bumped by businesslike persons
not even embarrassed to see my sex dreams dangling

a cross-eyed black man
in an overcoat like a brown jellabah
the stores selling cassbahs of trinkets
the street jingling like ankle bells on belly dancers
horns honking in traffic echo horns in the Metropole
North African whores "black meat" he promises
holed up in reeking cheap hotels
off Broadway productions.

I want to be alone with this city
with this 42nd Street Hong Kong crowd
massing like colored banners weaved by dragons
the relation of the street with windows
glassy metallic slow ripples in wind
I am stoned on city.

People flooding out of movie theatres
discussing camera angle phenomenologies immense
and radiant   Christ, it's all too much
I am surrounded   overwhelming floods
their electric looks!

IN the school I can say   nothing
we read St. Augustine
the talk is all neurosis this
and Oedipus that   or neo-platonic influences
pathologies of religious experiences

I want to ask
haven't you felt it
ain't you never gone cold turkey over sex?
You could chew plaster frescoes
depicting your own crucifixion.

I suffer both his Catholic knowing
the host of Christ
grace into the body
doing a dance for joy down the aisle
into the Jordan home of Jesus
Holy Spirit hovering wings of delight
and his Carthaginian swoons of pleasure

it is a feeling   a passion
he drunk and aphrodisiac hard-on for the atoms
of his people's lives
he feels his body expanding toward the universe
like everything is falling like a deck of cards
shuffled together
he sees the Oneness
suggested in the glittering animation of Kings and Queens
the connection between them
binding all merely visible worlds into a city of God.

But you cannot do   that
to people
no more can I.

I begin dreaming the faces of New Yorkers
are flowers framed architectual
in steel
        there is no way to reach
these rapid transit passengers
their faces are strong
fighting every day to keep from being conned.

In the 42nd Street underground
I see a blind man crippled
he drops his cigar box
the crowd stops to see if he can pick them up
sliding his fingers over the pavement
"Bastards!" I yell.

On the 242nd Broadway Express that night
another blindman with candy-striped cane tapping
and on the landing between cars
he stops, lifts his dark glasses
to tally the silver.

HOME in Southbridge on New Year's Eve
Anno Domini 1958
I am drunkenly raving about the symmetry
of Aquinas's proofs
to a friend who is driving me around town.

The whole world seems Medieval to me
I am imagining Times Square
the hundred thousand souls waving like algae
having flowed into that forum

I could watch it on tv   the lighted ball
descending   the thousands cheering Earth
into a new revolution   a strictly pagan charge with cosmos
the prince in Washington would soon
send armies into North Africa

my old friends in the Army   boots at Dix
spit-shining their government issues
and the guy who was driving me just waiting for
his chance to satisfy himself by saying "You've changed."
Him living in suspense with this perfect girl
going to college "postponing immediate gratification
to achieve long-range goals" he says
sounding like a congress of plague ridden monks
intoning he tries to make some kind of intellectual
pact with me   that we are superior
to the soldiers and workers.

WHEN I walked in Globe Village
the rhythm of the Ames Worsted Mills
the cloth being warped and woofed
with a clack and a clack
the bobbins spinning   their threads eaten
by the looms   frames   shuttles
a finished product spewing out on rolls
like an endless textile tongue

people were working   all the summer windows
were opened in the heat   the men the women
worked   I could smell their sweat
they leaned out of doorways for a draught of air
and waved hello wishing they were young like me
and wanting me to have my rightful childhood.

The Quinebaug was dammed above the Globe
and the woolen plants poured their dyes
red and blue and green
                              and swimming in the river
I would come home clownish in mottled flesh.

All these things passed into me
and I am their loom
endless, endless
they dyed they weaved the patterns
these workers   eating supper at 5:30 with their families
in their homes on Hamilton Street

I felt they were my mothers and fathers too
adults   mysterious   smoking cigarettes
they would feed me I knew if I asked

I see these people in wet bathingsuits
on Sunday afternoon picnics at Cedar Lake
fully grown   erect   sharing their laughter.

My mind is sultry rainstorms on these
bricked castles on the river:
how can   how should   I deny them?

BUT in an atlas I see
all the highways, railways, steamship lines
airlanes
                    converging into New York City
the same as lines of electromagnetic force
as if true north had shifted
and sucked the energy of the planet
into the wounded mouth of America.

EVERY noon I go to the Metropolitan Museum
to stare at deKooning's *Easter Monday*
I see Christ's body in ice
frozen martyr steaks.

There's a man there
he's the art director of a Mad Av firm he says
tells me what the painting's all about
the death of religion   tethered to priests
marbled altars become whited sepulchures
the paint applied with sponges
the cross is overturned.

Walking down 5th Av under the bare ginko trees
Central Park in February late snows like Breughel festivals
kids sled down snowhills
and suddenly I am overmade   lost in New York City
the roses of these people's lives
have thorns   thorns
I bleed
            there's too much to know
I could turn to landscape.

IN the Heat-Wave Bar

"I am a Brazilian," she insists
"not one of your puerto rico persons,"
leaning her hip into me
her arm around my waist
the smoke and noise going around
with the blue lights.
"I must have champagne," she whispers.

"Ah," she says, "watch this one.
She is a very great artiste."

There in the spotlight
is this beautiful woman making love to a black crepe doll.
She kisses it   slow   and snakes it down her body   slow
then rubs it in her groin.
The joint is stark still.
Each roll of her hips draws deeper breaths
until the doll turns the trick and   she comes.

The stage goes dark
the drummer lights another cigarette:
by the time I turn around
the chick is with this high roller
in a $300 suit.

I lean on the bar
drinking depth charges   the whiskey shot glass
sinks to the boots of the beer
explodes
          In the back room
the women are dancing with girls

one comes drunken   weaving Gulf Stream
her hair I smell light dawns
her ass round

I reach and slip my arm around her waist
a long deep kiss   Floridas in my mouth
my shoulder screams
                    I turn
it is this dyke   has stabbed me
I deck her
            the bartender leaps   chasing me out
brandishing his ice-pick.

These encounters are sudden:
I feel like a man from an ignorant century.
The 242nd train rocks my blood
para bomba/para bomba/para bomba!

NEW YORK CITY stands impenetrably what it is
on that hard schist   a metamorphic finger
of some Appalachian orogeny

downtown brawny men in yellow hardhats
jackhammer the streets into black flakes
are these the only ones who can remake this city?

I am the son of the Six Nations too.

Drunk   kneeling on the sidewalk
sliding my hand over the concrete
of the mid-Manhattan fault

a cab-driver says to his fare
"Look at that nut,"
but I have found the wound of New York City
I am not what he said.
It is just another place to be lonely.

Build   destroy   in time-lapse vision
the towers of the city rise and fall
rapid   rapid   wires for reinforced concrete images
lie coiled on the dust
they rise like charmed snakes into the future.

ON the banks of the Hudson
it is wider than a hundred Quinebaug Rivers
and moves more silently   deeper far
freightboats chug on her rippling flesh
George Washington Bridge lit carnival
traffic whizzing into the mainland

and I am dancing on the Hudson
toward a Palisade looming
some girl waits for me

some days in the morning
the sky is blue in New York City
and I could dare
to love.

Newport Riot

THERE were lichen-covered boulders
and milky birches shimmering
the April sun

you sat with down-cast eyes
your arms around your knees while the breeze
blew your hair to auburn filaments

everywhere life was blooming and you
were trying not to say
you wanted a baby and a home.

You soiled your dress
with leaves and mud and I soiled
something between us
in asking for sex at a bad time.

Later   you walked home
and you wouldn't look at me.

OUTSIDE on the steps of "The Moorings"
the boats rocking at the wharves
she sits
   she won't even let me
light her cigarette now
"Goddamit!" I yell
     and she runs away
into the dark streets the music pouring
around her and she is lost.

I am standing in the sinkhole of time
not seeing how she wanted to be done with it

wouldn't let me do anything for her
because that would be another beginning
she didn't want
    wanting instead
to be free running to be free
her hair flowing in air as water.

An empty thump of my heart
knowing the afterburn of touch taken away
never to trace the magic of her
no more.

WHEN we found her in the street
with some strange guy   I ran up to her
pulled her away by the wrists

the guy said, "Let her go,"
and Clea told him she was crazy
was let out only for the weekends
had delusions she was Magdalene
went around finding Jesus to wash his feet
with her hair   it went down past her buttocks

a fiction   more true
she was laughing that abandoned way of women
who have seen escape escape
she sat down in the gutter
and it was then we saw her feet bleeding
from the broken glass in the street.

We talk   in the backseat
no more naked lovemaking   yes sweet she
comes and kisses me   the taste of my cock
on her lips   her body with my body

and all around the streets of Newport
the bars rock   jam ten deep   fights breaking out
the dancers   divebombers whistle in their blood
a riot building to break the decade open

about God and the taste of Christ's body
"I believe we are all sperm swimming
in the gysm of God," I said

"I don't mind listening to you," she said
"but don't touch me."

And if I had known I might have said
something to her   about the century
about me   like this:

A Sistine Chapel of Southbridge/The Endless Poem Merged

You want to know why I always seem
to be leaving   even when I've just blown in?
Or drunk
without the least sensation
stumbling stunstruck into black corners
burnt, nervetorn?
                              I can't say
except I question every night again asking
father, where are you?

I seem   to have
like untroubled dreams   moving images of his story
it goes on   without explanation   and leaves
not so much as a mood when I awake.
                                               Like
a child I am in corduroy pants   jacket
faded blue   sitting in the dirt backyard driveway
garage door trashbarrel doghouse chickenwirefence
the house of strangers paid to keep me

                                        the roar
the roar of bombers I remember most
father, mother, war
alone crying in the stranger's backyard
water drips slow from rain
twigs stand topping sand houses   the sun
where are you?

When my brother came home on leave from Parris Island
my mother sat in the kitchen   the breeze
billowed the curtain   and death touched her shoulder
as she rocked in fierce silence.

Still photograph   an oval
portrait   rouged cheeks retouched my father
and crossed American flags furled at the bottom
sailor hat   long thin neck   a boy really

pink innocence
                    the image   smokeblack seas
a 17-year-old deckhand   the convoys steaming
New York to Liverpool
                              at sea, a boy dragged to work at 14
the mills dreary as coffins
he wanted more
                    a union

        the boss beat him down by the power
        plant   the spray through the rainbow
        and when he woke he was blacklisted

the bulkheads all broke in
seawater dams gushing mountains of
O God I don't want to die!
water   water green and white   off the western coast
of England :   the Kaiser   Christ I hate his ass!

Down at the beach   Nantasket   Revere or Lashaway
the bathing suits   sashed   strapped   girls
incredible flatchest bobbed hair   curlhooked at the ears
wide runningboard sedan Buick roadcar
fifteen minutes before the danceland crashed
under the Charlestown rag
my father and mother left to go smooching along the Charles

        I used to wonder sometimes
        why should he want to tell me?
        Telling about his life   him
        teaching me to drive, goddamit
        me twenty years old
                I was told not to try
                getting my driver's license
                for a lot of years
                              the
                judge in
                chambers sus

            pended my sen
            tence   a year on pro
            bation
                        for stealing a Buick

I says to my Ma
"I don't even *know* him!"

        "I want you to know, many's the time I
        left this place," my father said,
        "I always hated Southbridge, always
        wanted to get away   get to the big time
        so after the war I stayed in New York
        a man stumbled into this hotel lobby
        couldn't speak a word of the English
        so I helps him   he was lost   spoke only the French
        so being Canuck by Christ he gives me a job

        he had a sugar planation in Haiti
        I had a white horse   would ride around
        watching the niggers work
                                but I had
        to get out of there
        his old lady got to   looking at me

        they had no kids
        nights the moon was white   big   God
        the niggers breathing heavy
        the frenchman would ride his stallion
        to a flaming lather

        she got drunk
        come into my room   I
        had
                to get out of there.

        In January I came ashore at New York
        in a panama suit

          pneumonia set in
          my Ma had to come get me
          so it was back to Southbridge.
          I hated that hold!"

I don't even *know* him, I said to my Ma
with him driving them trucks
coming home in the morning on Thursdays
sleeping till supper   tousled hair scratching his ribs
lighting a cigarette   pork chops fried potatoes   beans
leaning that rig of his toward Newark that night
coming back Saturday morning   going and coming
every other day through all the weeks of my boyhood
all the weeks of my life
                          the boys at the terminal
baptizing him Suitcase Joe
eating in diners   sleeping in a cheap hotel in Jersey
the *Morning Telegraph* for the morning line
Joe and Asbestos for the handicaps
driving down to Lincoln on his vacations
I knew it was like drink or some other pipe dream
he would win sometimes and when he hit the double
he felt elected   God was with him
and he would never die.

I had to defend myself against the heart attack
of my Ma
                "O dear God! He's going bad just like
                his brother."
                My brother telling me:
                "Six months to a year
                for assault with a deadly weapon."
                Marine belt buckle   he was a China Marine.
                "You should have seen 'em
                they took them communists out in the street
                tied 'em up and shot 'em in the back of the head

BAM   it was over
Them Chinese women, man,
good ginch.

At Parris Island a hundred an' eighty of us
started   and sixty made it through
if they didn't break your body
they broke your mind."

                              O yeah, brother, I said
                              I know   I feel like the
                              third generation into this
                              crummy century
                              but I'm only the second.

"What makes a mean sargeant mean?
I mean what combination of hereditary and environmental
factors coalesce to form his character?"

          "Look   the meanest bastards you'll ever know
          were just born that way."

Brawling with the 4Fs back home:
          "The women used to hang out at Dragon's Cafe
          paid you good money to bang 'em
          hell, big spenders   buy you clothes
          all on the checks from their husbands
          dying in them goddam steaming jungles
          fuck 'em and beat the shit out of 'em

          six months trying to stay sane
          the goddam junkies crying and crying
          all night the guards come and beat the
          shit out of 'em
          but they just keep screaming

          or the queers   catch you in a stall alone
          you gotta have guts   half kill
          the bastards to make 'em leave you alone."

52

"He's going bad just like his brother,"
she cried   until slit silence   polka dots focus deep

You wound up taking off
small wonder something you sensed drove you away
home was mother and death:

      "Look, look," my father said
      lifting his trousers
      the massed scartissues on his knees
      Christ I cut my knees too feeling
      "West Virginia coal mines
      I worked for scrip   fought for a union
      deep down in the mines you work on your knees
      with a little pick hacking away:
                                people
      were shot
      they hired strikebreakers   I
      was there   saw
      a woman lose her baby 'cause she hadn't no milk for it"
"That why you peddled milk during the Depression?"
      "maybe so."

Some day my father'd be a regular man at the track
have a couple of thousand in reserve
make maybe sixty a day
just betting the sure thing
going with the smart money

      my brother was the same
      dreaming Las Vegas as the big time
      the damn desert of the dollar
      cool clear money

me stumbling around Southbridge eating in diners
talking to greek cooks about Aristotle
and the pre-Socratic scientists
dreaming about the source of all Being

53

    you loved me then
fire   air   land   water
the names ring   Anaxagoras Anaximander Thales Heraclitos
how many times did the Quinebaug flame
in Heraclitos's vision?
wondering why there's something rather than nothing.

Working in a mill with my brother
going to college at night .
reading Milton, for God's sake.

Father, where are you?

            "Working on phone lines for Southern Tel
                stringing wire down through Georgia
            you can't ever trust them niggers"
            lifting his shirt up   the scar   white
            and hideous   long across his gut
            "one of them gave me this with a razor."

I knew too long afternoons
in the dust of late September
I stepped on a guy's outstretched arm in a pileup
it felt weird   giving under my weight
as it broke
and I knew   being center   the middle guard broke my
face punching all afternoon my face caked with death
me crying wanting to kill complaining to the ref
"You wanna play the game, kid?
Or you wanna tell me my job?"

My father and brother were there wondering
was I addled? could I tell what day? what game?
was I nuts or just punchy?

Am I nuts? or just punchy?
I suspect I ain't nuts enough
you see   you who think me cruel.

Didn't they give a "scholarship" to break people?

I want to get it down
to make the words transparent, don't you see?
That's like the observation room
see-through mirrors
so anyone can see how it's being done.
If I achieve an "aesthetic distance" I suspect
I'm playing their games
like having wars to make Art out of.

My first love, dear one
the wildcat woman and when she said "come"
I came trailing like a dog
and my friend he said to me
"Man, she was fucking for us all,"
me remembering that pine world we found
"Let me tell you though"   my friend said
"I found out what guts is:
at Bragg I mean   I used to think it was
fighting   Some guy crowd you you know what
or your buddies need you around for a gangfight
you're there
                        but when I run out 5:30 in the morning
I couldn't take it   the guys in the company
all run by singing Airborne!   Airborne!
I thinks   I thinks   them guys   they ain't going
to finish and I don't finish:
so I got the idea
                        guts I says to myself
is finishing something you start.
Am I punchy?
                        We used to play this game
to see which stick would hit DZ first
we'd collapse the chute with the lines
and fall dead   deep   deep   toward the earth   like
waiting long   long into a girl with the come
a gamble waiting in your balls to spurt out

you never know just when

you hadda judge   letting the lines pop
the chute pooled and you settle to ground
on your feet like a cat
the first on your stick with only money to burn

the whores in Columbia stinking sweet
after the bars   jukeboxes   multicolored
country and western shitkicker music, man,
whining in your ears
                        you stand weaving in the mensroom
pissing all over, your cigarette tasting damn good
deep in your lungs
the buzzing in your head bleeding memories
you smell the come
green shades half down a breeze lifts the shade gently
you puke
            the brig   call your name and number
all present and accounted for."

And here you are wondering and past
wondering why
I am such a mean prick
and I speak of these things now, too late
though God knows they wouldn't have made a difference

you wonder out loud how I could
just drive down the road like my father taught me
what the weight of these places are
in my life   and the places and what
happened in them   justify in some regard
saying: I was born that way.

I could play my horn drunkly in winter
up by the airport   the place we first made love
the air so cold it freezes my valves:
so what?

Play   blow it all out   drive the hard bop
battling the hard time   I could tell you now
listen to Bird!   the bastard knows too much
when drunk I hear him I take to smashing walls
with my fists   he knows that much

devil he dreams time fusing the spare parts
left him   shoving them together
he makes a melody   I am a mad rage in icestorms
too drawing everything into me for fusion.

I heard your God
roar in the waves of Massachusetts Bay
the Voice came rushing over me
I stumbled around; the rocks cut my feet
people yelled with torches down the beach
I heard   they're yelling for me.

Let me go, let me go: I'm not nuts, just punchy.
Deny it if you can in yourself.

Like Bird remake a world you can't live with
without getting punchy.
By hurting you I located the hurting in me.

If I could say these things to you
if I could stand in Copley Square with you
and point to the Prudential building
now   years later

all them stories stacked one on top of the other
and we could look straight down through
if the floor was glass and all the people
their lives
see? father?

Then watch
you walk down along the Charles to see

the lovers smooching
the earth is lifting the stars over the city
the sky is clear means maybe you'll be too come tomorrow

you hear voices in the distance
and you want   I say now
to live.

AFTER thirty-six hours
the whole drunken street
the city is plastic
the sundown lean-against-the-door cool

before the corrals of sleep
before the Army raids our border
before they butcher us in the red cock-aching hallucination
of Independence Day

lie in the grassy median strip
until showtime   the bishop
is preaching tonight

see the girl with the red dress on
she really knows   how to shake that thing
o baby

it's that he gets the notes to bend
that we are stuck with him
having sweated his rushes

we do not ask when is this shit going to end
the money-men of Newport still have
Ray in chains   there's a track up his forearm
that reaches back four hundred years

we want and we want and we want

FREEBODY Park
well-dressed ticketholders   thousands are in
walking on the outfield sipping beer in waxed cups

the music spurts from sixfoot speakers
and along the line stretching for streets
and blocks seventhick   the word that

the cops have closed the gates
the ground trembled with anger
cops bopped down streets pushing people
into the Boulevard with nightsticks

and we see them becoming one
and in the center a young man with a bigpipe
straight from Culloden
marched up to the green doors

the crowd stormed them
beer cans full heavy fly
bloody headed cops fall
nightsticks crack back

firemen spray us with highpressure hoses
we steal a firetruck and spray them back
we're up on a roof of a garage and they teargas us

the fight goes on and we retreat

Later, like Peter when the cock crew thrice
we denied any part of it
the Mayor and his Vigilantes
caught up with us

"What cha doin?"
"Eatin Cheese its."
"OK, you're goin to the station, ya wise bastard!"

In the squad car between badges
"You wanna cheese it?"

60

Jack Kerouac's Funeral

WHERE'S St. Jean Baptiste Church?
a sunoco gas-station
at the end of the Rt. 495 cut-off
DOWNTOWN LOWELL the sign

Oh, Saint John da Baptis'!
Hey Harry (over the door H.H. Johnson)
where's saint john's
                              a guy draining the oil
of a car on the lift yells
jus' keep goin' til you can't go no more
turn lef' an' you're on mer-mak street
that's frenchtown, up abouta halfamile

the second part is
finding jean baptiste in a rundown
wounded neighborhood
gaping spaced lots waiting for urban renewal
like an old hag waiting for false teeth

stop in a coffeeshop
cupacoffee at the counter, readin' the Lowell *Sun*

          suffering a massive hemorrhage
          a former Lowell *Sun* sportswriter
                              French literary
          prizes *Maggie Cassidy,* which tells of
          his life and times, in fictional form, at
          Lowell High School
                    On the Road
          "beat" refers to beatific
                              a bridge
          between the Lost Generation . . . and the heirs of
          the Beat Generation, the hippies (sure)

          educated at Lowell . . . went on to
          Columbia in New York where he played football
          (me too, me too)

guy comes in
give me the two crull-er, eh? an' coff-ee to go.
frenchtown
         I thinks of maggie, the scene where
he's sittin' on the can and she's blowin' him
tryin' to get him to stay home insteada goin' off
to college, he wantin' the city, writin'
leavin' her and the life of a railroad brakeman behind

yeah, I thinks, this is where
the tenement three-deckers
the backlot pickup baseball games in the twilight
before the mothers callin' kids home
to fridaynight fish fries
and the omnipresent sacred heart of Jesus calendar
hung on the inside of the bathroom door
in french naming the saintsdays
are
    an' wow here's the merrimack river
rocks and the riverwater's in the three channels
Jesus! I thinks, just like
southbridge I knew it

across the street from the church
a young guy says, They're goin' to have it
at eleven   I says Where's the home
(meaning where'd the kerouacs live) but
he says up the street at archambeault's

so the third part is
in archambeault's funeral home
where I come back into the real french-canadien
idea of class
        a room marked MR JACK KEROUAC
and there he is, in the casket

the place is empty except for this
like maybe crazy college kid standing against the wall

64

with a funny smile on his lips
I kneels and prays (one for cynthia) looks and
jesus jack you are still there, your
soul? yes, soul, is still there

you look mighty like my uncle pete
in your bowtie and check jacket, rosary beads
clasped in your hands (badly crinkled)
and your classic features, greek statue lips
long straight nose
                    noble, remember?
WORK LOVE SUFFER Kerouac motto
next to the bier a coupla dozen roses shaped into a valentine
the red satin ribbon bearing the gold legend
GUARD THE HEART
                    who sent it?

guy comes in   whips off his winter jacket
plunks down on the pew   wrings his hands
sighs loud tears O JACK I MADE IT JACK

mrs kerouac, stella, comes in
the guy comes up with rheumy words
are you mrs kerouac   I'm VERY sorry
holding her right hand in both of his
until she pulls it away

tight jaw and dry eyes
deep lines and black depression trenches
in her face, the veil, anguish
like shot in the stomach but tryin' not to cry out

Ginsberg comes in with Corso
(a long navyblue coat rasputin wore)
allen stands bending at the waist talking
to mrs kerouac saying how he and gregory
will make a movie about the funeral
and she looks up she says

Do what you want
but I never want to see you again

arrggh!
and he bows (quiet guru) and goes to corso
and the sound of the goddam camera whirring

out on the street I hears the merrimack
rushing over its rocks
standin' on the high bridge the wind
bright with october morning blue sky
                                        I hear
boys in bathingsuits yelling running barefooted
over 1935 rocks
a lowell tech kid walking by says
don't jump   christ, do I look that bad
                                        I see
jack straying along the river thinkin'
about serpentine monster in the core of the planet
getting ready to rise, its sulphurous snake-eyes springing
into the atmosphere of lowell and rising
like a rocket menacing the cellstructure of the universe

it rises and rises
until it fall into innocent atoms
                            poor emerson
only dr sax KNOWS

there's a three-decker
with clotheslines of sheets flapping white
and jack is up there
with a jug of wine, only
it's the GREAT AMERICAN NIGHT and stars
like headlights cruising down turnpikes of eternity

jack is gettin' a little high
lookin' from off that rooftop to the river
thinkin' of his old buddies

sampas maybe, thinkin' of who and what
regrets, finally remorse
loving God in the mountains of washington
burnt out on his friends in frisco
buddha burns in the shacks of berkeley

go on loving, dying somewhere between
the artist and the man   take your choice
be a artist or a human person
                              the artist
will make a movie of his friend's deathtime
I thinks, judge not lest ye be judged
ginsberg is just then driven into the parkinglot
behind the church
judge not WORK LOVE SUFFER

the next part is the funeral
father morrisette speakin' with that fren ch'accent
of the sins of israel (judge not)
so beautiful he prays
please Father forgive your servant jack
for any sins he may have committed in this life

in black vestments with gold trim
the church high vaulted ceilings, paintings of the saints
and jean, john, jack baptizing in the jordan the young christ
Are you the messiah?
No, I am but a voice crying in the wilderness.

The eulogy
          jack lived around here and came to this church
          even when he was a boy he used to come
          to the rectory and talk about how he wanted to write
          to express the feelings he had in words

          we encouraged him
          he left us and went out and made a great name
          and wrote his writings

I read his books
some say his books are indecent
but I could see that they were a great force for good
because jack had a vision
of the freedom of the human spirit
and spoke against every form of bullying he met

now he is at rest

said father morrisette and I guess everybody just knows
jack's going to heaven to be with gerard

around the casket shaking the censor
incense rising to the rhythm of the bells
holy water beading up on the bronze
the old man with the crucifix leading the procession to the doors

the casket down the steps
into the tv camera
denise in cloth coat, creeley
a reporter takes jimmy breslin's statement

and the last part is
out at the cemetery down along the avenues of the dead

mrs kerouac no tears not once
the priest, I am the life the resurrection
tv cameras churning   corso's camera whirring
mrs kerouac leaving as soon as the final
syllable of the glory be evaporates

ginsberg handing the camera to creeley
he using the one eye into the eyepiece
a shot of corso ginsberg laying a yellow carnation on the casket
the eternal celluloid record
                              I guess
creeley is another true artist

drivin' down south home through towns
stow and bolton and marlboro I hears jack sayin'
all american authors are insane   you gotta be crazy
to be a writer in this country

angleheaded hipsters in the starry dynamo
of the night all mad for life generating this
spontaneous bop prosody

exactly one year before
I write
            dear jack,
                        please don't die
                        write more books instead

now he is at rest
and I'm goin' home to make a poem
of jack's deathtime
I'll just keep goin' til I can't go no more
turn lef' and there he'll be

Crying in the Cheap Seats

IN Provincetown Cynthia and I
and the Wolf talk in "The Fo'c's'le"
to a kid from Persia

he's on cocaine
wearing an overcoat from Peru
llamas graze   and shedding it alternately
talking about "going through changes."

"I find no peace and all my war is done
I fear and hope, I burn and freeze like ice"
he said Peter Lorre nervous laughing.

I breathe blue flame listening to
his conflagration
consumed with love for a century.

Out in the street it rains
Pentecostal   the Wolf declares he is
a religious figure
"Beware the heart," he says,
"it is wicked and above all deceitful."

I am a brand lighting the street
the houses are where the sane people are
and even the Persian in his cocaine
Zoroastrian changes
Ahura Mazda/Ahriman
sees a glimpse of Eden.

In bed that night with Cynthia
I wonder what it is like to be earth and water
sleeping with flame
my brain churning like a North Atlantic engine.

MISCARRIAGE

That cold stillness in the house
when I came home
was the same as when my brother went to war
and my mother rocked and rocked
in fierce silence.

Here and now
my wife had miscarried
was sick
heart mind and body.

No words could have explained
consoled encouraged
or given the bravery with which
she cleaned the house.

WHEN the nurse brought him round
to the door marked NO ADMITTANCE
to let me touch him instead of just
gawking through the window

a flash hit me
and I remember thinking:
God!   A new person!

My wife   my wife
she puts me down.

The house is too cold
the baby cannot sleep.

Her swollen breast aches
she bites her lip.

I bite my lip too
worrying about   words.

IN a dream
I am a teacher in a grey schoolroom
grey light in at the windows
I speak a grey lesson.

There is a game
my students demand
I must say   why
the lesson.

they argue   deny   rebel
walk out.

Why should they not?
I am whittled of chalk
my voice is fingernails on blackboards.

In my dream the empty room
and the empty feeling in my gut
makes me walk out too.

IN Southbridge nations find their plots of land
plant backyard vineyards   erect churches
build pavilions of dance and courtship.

Greeks, Albanians, Roumanians dance
for courtship   the young people
holding hands

the leader   Stepho, I can still see you
waving his handkerchief   spinning   leaping
presenting the dance line to ancient Gods

the grandparents making matches
sitting and sipping *raki*
dreaming of golden orthodox
rituals with satin white ribboned rings
and the priest dancing thrice around the altar
the masque of marriage teaching the young
the form of its dance
binding and flowering mystery on mystery.

THE African spear and the staves of the Steppes
are hurled each night for my seldom sleeping
ships cannon coastal cities.

I am an assassin in a decade of assassination
outrage   confusion   exorcism will not do
I become a Hashshashin
murdering the Christian heroes of the Western World.

The hero who is killed in the morning
hears wind rustling reeds by the Nile
birds take flight in the Okeefenokee

the Greek ships sail on
the Antartic mountains sail on under clouds
the egg in the womb of every woman in
the Western World emits a cry.

IN the Freebody Park vortex once again
years after the riot
with my wife and my old girl.

I am drunk to boot from Murphy's "Jive Samba"
shouting down woodenchair rows
for the Wolf
I am listening to my old girl
tell the sorrows of loving a junkie.

She is beautiful and I hold her hand
and I hold my wife's hand
she *needs* me my squeeze says

the fog comes in
Joe Williams singing out of the blue Newport haze
"Nobody loves me: nobody seems to care."
I am stumbling around smashed singing:
"Come with me, if you want to go to Kansas City."

I am crying in the cheap seats
people in the stands pissed off
trying to hush me
"Why'd j'come if you weren't goin' to listen to the music:
ain't nuthin' sacred to this bastard."
The girl who gave me a handkerchief
takes a second look and calls me a phony.
I guess she means I'm just havena jag
knowing yesterday is gone.

Years later at the new jazz location
a guy comes up to me and my wife and two sons
and says: "Say, aren't you the guy
who went around shouting the name of some animal
at Freebody Park?"

I am a legend.

I walk out into the winter night
to think about Kazantzakis' "Cretan glance"

and the endless poem brings me to
Breen's Bar in Worcester
with friends in a booth drinking
talking
            one friend says Dylan Thomas
is *the* great modern bard
the other says Thomas is "just
a manner of speech"
and he begins to roll out carolling syllables
loud as the bartalk   the barflies buzzing
to hear him   matching the participial momentum
of Dylan's Welsh mind tumbling down into the harbor.

"Jesus Christ!" the first one says,
"if I had one tenth the talent
you're just pissing away I'd be up in my room
writing like a bastard:
what the hell are you doin'
drinkin' your life away!"

"Let me alone, then," the second one says,
"I am what I am
I can't and won't be anything to please you
or anyone else."
                The endless poem
is a long walk toward Cretan caves:
something about death
something about facing God and death
and all the unanswered questions
with courage and without insolence.

*I*N the endless poem
I wonder sometimes what the connection is
between the poem and the world.

Do I expect the world
not to kill or maim me?
not explode my house of ecstasy?

Do I expect an end to the murder of children
their bodies thrown in ditches
ripped by phosphorous bullets?

This endless poem is a song: someone
somewhere hears its syllables.

The melody makes moments yet alive
and makes us frightened too of other harms
we do ourselves
                                as when, if
we would wait alone for execution scared into silence
and never make this fragile and temporary music.

        In the endless poem
we are in death row: it is vast
and   contains
the world.

A Time for Breaking

NIXON SENDS COMBAT UNITS INTO CAMBODIA
TO ATTACK COMMUNISTS' STAGING AREA
American advisor on a South Vietnamese troop
carrier near Chipou, Cambodia, yesterday (AP)

He looks back, his
teeth are bright, his eyes
advise the boyish glee of blitzkreig to ARVN   soldiers

why is this man smiling?
do the machineguns erect on armored personnel
carriers, the whip antennae
fluttering flags gaily overhead
portend the TOTAL VICTORY?

Walk on the campus with newspaper in hand
the faculty the students gather in little
groups on the 1st of May to shake their heads
and talk and talk and fall to silence

even the wind protests more loudly

we walk alone clutching our guts
crying   what can I do?
nothing

              TROUBLE ON CAMPUS
Students at Ohio State University in Columbus
facing the bayonets of National Guardsmen (AP)

May 4th 1970 6:30 PM Walter Cronkite says
four Kent State students have been shot to death
        by National Guardsmen
Cynthia stands in the kitchen doorway, crying
a hot flash washes over me
it's all over now   the time is coming
a time of breaking
I can feel some organ rupturing in my spirit

the city editor of the *Telegram & Gazette* says
yes, we have their names
ALLISON KRAUSE SANDY SCHEUER
JEFFREY GLENN MILLER WILLIAM SCHNEIDER

    BRING THE WAR HOME the sign says   says
    Nixon: "When dissent turns to violence
    it invites tragedy."
    the writing is on the wall

In memory of these people
out of a sense of grief at their loss
a day of mourning tomorrow, May 5, 1970

all students to join in an assembly
the slayings the invasion protest
we wrote that at Leicester Junior College
after I gave Wayne and Charlie and Dan
the list of the names of the dead and we stood
in room 106 Knight Hall, shaken, knowing
the time is coming

    bright October 15th 1969 morning
    students sitting on the steps
    of the white Unitarian Church
    Rev. Samuel May's church, the one
    they froze him out of on account of
    his relentless abolition sermons

    before reading poetry I recalled
    Arthur Miller on the floor
    of the 1968 downhome Democratic National
    Convention after hearing some Texas
    representative berating students
    at Lincoln Park to the wild applause
    of the delegates
                   he said this is
    the only issue

not war not poverty not racism
the older generation hates its own
wants to see them dead

the young are the conscience of America
and America wants to kill its conscience
I said that morning and now the time is coming
we know it now   there'll be more killings

At Clark University the Black Student Union
and SDS walked out screaming NO!
Denise Levertov made a fist at the crowd and
        called for a revolution
the BSU and SDS marched back in waving fists and
banners like fists   jumping on stage
seizing the microphone   screaming
        but they were back in the hall
and joy hit the ceiling   the movement would live!

At Leicester in the student center
Don played guitar and the students shouted
STRIKE STRIKE STRIKE STRIKE
Rev. Jerry Morgan called for prayer and asked
them please to examine their consciences
but the fear was on them
I said this is serious business
you've got to think about why you're doing it

they marched in their darkness by torchlight
singing give peace a chance
                        the time is coming
even the president of the college could see it
the drunk ones screamed LET'S KILL A COP
LET'S ALL DIE TONIGHT LET'S BURN
THE PRESIDENT'S HOUSE DOWN
the president's wife scared alone in the house
and someone tried to throw a torch
finally Dan got them to go away

Cynthia and I tried to sleep both of us were
scared   laying together we talked of the end
of everything the house the job the education
the planned future the degrees the money
the security the cars the   world
everything   except the love the marriage the
children
            it's all over now and her parents
would not approve of what we are thinking

I keep having visions of the president's wife
of people breaking into our house, killing
hard times, hard times on the country
over and over again in my head
no sleep

I saw John the next morning
do you support the student strike, John?
no, he said and that was it
I felt like I was falling thru space
the sides being drawn

the students were sitting around the center
stunned   they hadn't ever seen a group become
a mob and guilt was on their faces
they were going to castrate themselves and the
strike for contrition

the faculty convenes to consider the proposal
for amnesty for strikers
they are in the mood to call the strike a   moratorium
Wayne is furious   it's not a moratorium
it's a STRIKE
        the faculty wants to help in its
        way   for some though the only urgency is
        to complete their silly byes
        classes to go on for those who
        "want an education"

some don't understand   some understand
they just want to crush the strike

like when Wayne talked to them about the war
and changing the school
he ran outside and vomitted from the vision of
        dying children
but some thought he was just
"too sensitive"

and indeed the strike almost dies until on
the 6th of May students from Worcester
picked their spirits up   Eric was striding
up and down the aisles shouting turning people
off with his revolutionary playacting
I pulled him aside
                        cut it out, will you?
I said you're acting like a two-bit demagogue
and you aren't helping

he stood there really put down

the students voted to strike and immediately
half of them took off for a long weekend
that's all it meant to them

later that night I went over only
to find Eric and hug him and beg him
to forgive me for being so harsh
and it was the first time I ever had
touched a student and everybody who was there
working on the phones or the typewriters
writing petitions stopped and was watching
and afterwards Dan said that I had really
given the kids something and it was better
than giving them a grade and it was better
than showing them the missing element in
The Scarlet Letter is foregiveness instead of

hardheartedness   because this is it
the time is coming
the writing is on the wall
love has got to conquer

in red paint the writing is on the wall
at UMASS everything is changed
at Bartlett Hall a man tells me that, no, I
will not get a teaching assistantship
the federal government has cut back on aid
to education
                    the doors are closing on me
so to hell with worrying about myself
there's too much to learn now

in a lecture hall Leslie Fiedler says
that if there is a revolution
it will be socialist
and if it is it will oppress the university
he ends with this image of himself
in some classroom in a totalitarian city giving
a lecture on *The Tempest* to no one

next day Friday the 8th
Bernard Kaplan speaks at Leicester
I keep wanting to ask him to give a psycho-
analysis of Nixon   but we all know

outside this kid comes up to me
saying how his father is going to disown him
for pledging to give up classes even if it means
he won't graduate
he's already selling my hydroplanes he said
and suddenly this guy in a Palm Beach businessman's
suit comes up jabbing his finger at me

you his teacher   no   you his advisor   no
you still teaching your classes   yes   how can you

instigate my son to throw away his future
but you don't take any risks   I didn't put your son
up to this, ask him if you want to
Dad he didn't push me into anything
I made the choice and the guy's yelling now
and Kaplan comes up and tries to calm the guy down
but he walks away and stops   yelling, is this the
kind of people you want insteada your family
is it? Come back and talk with us said Kaplan
if I come back there I'll belt you in the mouth
YEAH YEAH BELT US IN THE MOUTH DAD!
THAT'S ALWAYS THE WAY TO SOLVE THINGS
ISN'T IT?

so I said look you can come and live with us
yes, old families are breaking up now
new families are being born
this is a baptism said Kaplan

all this time very little sleep
Cynthia and I talk every night till dawn
my aunt calls to say my father's had
a massive heart attack

Cynthia's old friend calls
tell how her husband had her going to
counselling for two years and now she knows
it's him that needed it all along
because he *hates* her   everything she does
pisses him off he's in a constant rage at her
it's the end arriving on schedule
one more world coming apart

we talk about Cambodia and the nightly news
shows American soldiers blowing up bunkers
and one of my Vietnam veteran students hints
that a low-yield A-bomb went off by accident
he felt the shock-wave on a hill near Khe Sanh

91

Cynthia calls in mid-week
crying Phil and Dee Dee have broken up
she reads this letter it says that they
are happier being separated
that they were going to these group sessions
and discovered they loved each other
but that they were into unbreakable habits
of hurting each other in terrible ways
Phil quit his job teaching high school in
Brooklyn and they went to live in a commune
and it all went to pieces
Dee went off to upstate N.Y. with this
19-year-old kid
                        we ate supper that night
and it was in the air   the world is coming apart
the marriages made around the time of ours
are breaking up O smile on your brother
everybody get back together
and love one another right now

so then on Friday the 15th my aunt called
to say my father had died after a ten-day
stretch in the intensive care ward
that is they took him out and he died
so next morning there I am in a 727
jet flying seven miles above America
the whole northeast in cloud the sun shining
on middle America and I think of my father
how he loved America the greatest most
exciting gamble in history   a union man
all his life   I used to show him statements
very much like his own in the *Manifesto*
and kid him saying he was a communist
and he would get peeved and threaten to
belt me in the mouth

the rocky mountains the snow the star-shaped
clusters and then the desert the southwest

the redearth clay my aunt and brother next to
me, him the past commander of the VFW local
he'd never approve of my thoughts
and I think about the kid, the one whose father
would in rage disown him   how one day he came
with head bowed and said how he went home
and found that his sister is pregnant
and he has to promise his father
he'll finish his degree so his father won't have
a heart attack with his son a radical
and I wanted to judge him harshly but Eric
showed me how not to and here I was
keeping my mouth shut just like the kid
because even if these people do trust Nixon
and want to destroy the North Vietnamese (evil)
you still love them, like they have this
thing of the heart you feel like it's blackmail
but you can't do anything they are your flesh
        and blood

or when I saw my mother and she asked me
would I go with her to church on Sunday
I said yes of course I will even though
I've said I've put that away like a dead host
in a golden monstrance deep in my mind

her sitting in a wheelchair crippled
from a stroke her right half paralyzed
and she can't read anymore (her pleasure)
all she can do is live in the shadow silence
of her aphasia

we arrange to have the wake on Monday
night   what?   only one night?
yes that's the way they all do it now, Mom
it's better for everyone involved
but she knows she's being hussled

93

the three brothers from the East
we go out with the brother-in-law retired
Navy chief and he drives us south down
Linda Vista to Camino del Rio to Ocean Beach
wants to show us hippies on the beach
he drives by and doubles back and drives by again
I wonder why   is it he's afraid his kids will
be seduced by these people? what?
and we saw young kids in navy fatigues at
the Naval Training Center looking lonely
my brother-in-law extolling the virtues of
the military life
the jets streaking overhead   their exhaust
        covering the city
everything smells of war in San Diego

down Broadway we see downtown signs
BILLIARDS BOWLING DANCING
GO GO TOPLESS GIRLS and BEAVER MOVIES
CIVILIAN CLOTHES FOR HIRE
YOUR CREDIT IS GOOD WITH US

we walk slowly into the Church of the
        Immaculata with my mother
the mass begins   a folk band
the priests singing down the aisles
        THE KING OF GLORY COMES, THE NATION
        REJOICES   OPEN UP THE GATES BEFORE
        HIM, LIFT UP YOUR VOICES
there's these little red booklets saying
        CELEBRATE
my eyes are fixed on a blue gold-starred dome
and I'm floating there in a child memory
in the little book it says:
        WHY DO YOU STAND THERE?
        looking up into the sky . . .
        Jesus will come again!
could I believe that?

LOVE HAS NO ROOM FOR FEAR
RATHER   PERFECT LOVE
DRIVES OUT FEAR

Liturgy of the Word (in gothic lettering) :
THIS IS IT :
if you live by the Spirit . . . you will live.
All who are led by the Spirit of God
are the sons of God . . .
the Spirit itself gives
witness, together with
our Spirit
here is this miracle of change
and all I'm thinking of is the hold of the past
like old friend came east to take a teaching job
at Harvard and he shows up at the house
in a rented red car and mod clothes
smoking ceegars like Albert the Alligator
and what do I do? I take him out drinking
and playing pool in Tillie's roadhouse
'cause I want to get back to where we last had
fun   all I do is revert, bring back old miseries
with Cynthia, keep him up till dawn
trying to pump a free analysis out of him
when there's nothin that bad wrong that saying
I KNOW WHO I AM I AM A POET MAN A POET
wouldn't solve if I could just get free to say it
if I wasn't scared of quitting my job and writing
if I wasn't scared of what my aunt my mother
who are so proud of me that I'm a junior college
teacher   part of an ESTABLISHMENT
getting paid good money
live in a big white federalist house
if I could cure the paranoid monster inside me

here I am in the Immaculata Church
and nothing much has changed   except
this still photograph of students falling

95

puffs of white smoke from rifles commencing
a time of breaking   a time of photographic
hells of funeral corteges and long black trips
of mourning of madhouse jumbles of death
death and grief and disaster from Dallas to
Mylai to Memphis   something is breaking

my father is dead   the mortician and his helper
have pumped his veins full of death fluid
do the same fluids circulate in Nixon's brain?
And at least one of the people who holds me
back is gone   he cannot censure me now
why not be free of them all, haul away the
bonds, be free of the brothers and sisters
the governments
          THIS IS IT: if you live by the Spirit . . .

the priest preaches a sermon about peace
he doesn't come out against the war
but it's about as far as he can go in San Diego

          I speak of PEACE
          and they are ready for WAR!

back home at my sister's we eat
and take off for Tijuana   to Caliente, right on!
horses in the afternoon
I'm shamed to think I'm here in Mexico
knowing I'm not doing anything to comfort
my mother and I don't even like gambling
though my father was a gambler all his life
and I can hear him saying   don't mourn for me,
gamble!

my brother has a horse in the 8th
on the far turn his horse moves into 3rd
COME ON SIX! COME ON SIX!
WHIP THAT HORSE! WHIP THAT HORSE!

96

I looked into his eyes and he was gone
just like my father   he throws the ticket
on the ground   a loser

we eat lobster tails and filet mignon
at the Jai Lai Palace
my brothers and sister really put it to me
did I approve of student violence?
did I lead an insurrection?
    what could I say?
outside we see an Indian woman with baby
just as we're getting into the Thunderbird
MAHNEY MAHNEY FOR BABY
did we wish she'd just go into the desert
somewhere out of sight

back at Caliente for the dog races
we play a few but it's the craziest place
nobody bets a straight $2 bet
it's all these street-of-dreams parleys
quinellas and 4—9s and 5—10s
everyone wants to make $50,000

I go to the jai lai with my brother-in-law
the pelota whizzing against the wall
the logic of the game   the easy serve
the harder return   the harder slam
    to the back wall
the all-in-one-motion recovery   the drive
the quick slam into the corner
the unplayable carom

my sister and brother show up and she tells us
the story of this Mexican woman who took
someone's seat   the usher came to kick her out
YOU CAN'T DO THIS   I AM A MEXICAN
CITIZEN! I PAY FOR MY SEAT!
my sister said the woman was really vicious

because when she laughed at her (what else can
I do?) for some unaccountable reason
she started screaming she'd tear her eyes out
really crazy people, she said

we go down into the cheap bar section
god, the smell of vomit is like solid
encrusted for a century
the little frying stands where tortillas sizzle

the only ones who live in the Spirit
are the mariachi musicians roaming thru
the streets   2 trumpets guitars and fiddlers
meeting with each other talking laughing
laying one song after another on each other
they have these little coffee joints
and they play and hug each other dancing
drinking wailing digging each other

in a strip joint the girls stand on display
roll their hips a little   they are so tired
it's all too stupid
                        out on the streets
the hawkers in doorways smoking cigars
WE HAVE WHAT YOU ARE LOOKING FOR

the next day it's out to El Camino Real
Cemetery   which is OK because my father was
a truck driver
                        we talk of the insurance
money but there is the mystery of the $500
he borrowed from the Beneficial Finance Co.
just before he went into the hospital and died
no one can figure out where it went
but it is in essence the mystery of his life

then the afternoon the chapel
my mother my aunt brothers sister sitting

looking at him   he's almost handsome
I said Mom I remember best the picture of him
with his sailor suit on   can I have it?
and with her halting speech and tears
she said we ah bur-hurn'dit 'ca-hause
he got to wh-where he d-hidn't w-hant it
he, he was, he was y-houng, you know
he was . . . only seven . . . seven . . .
(seventeen?) yes, when he w-hent in and and and
in 19 . . . 1918 . . . when the w-har was o-
ver he j . . . just wa . . . . walked away
y-hears after we . . . after we were
m-harried he g-hot some papers on it

and she started to cry she said I d-hidn't
mean to . . . to tell you

outside my sister smoking fiercely said
in his last two years he became a fanatic
about the Catholic Church   like he
even believed that that was what's behind
the Vietnam War   that they were trying to
exterminate all the Catholics

finally when Pat comes in and hugs my mother
she really starts to cry for the first time
(does anybody notice she's not in the family?
and what does that say about us?)
my sister collapses after weeks of worry
it all hangs there in the flower-scented air
my brother said I'm glad you were with her
I couldn't have done it

Fr. O'Sullivan with a brogue contemplates
the five agonies of Christ in the rosary
speaks of the consolation of His death and
sufferings   Gethsemane to Golgotha
HOLY MOTHER OF GOD PRAY FOR US

NOW and AT THE HOUR OF OUR DEATH

and the funeral itself
I wanted to rise up and deliver a eulogy
rather than sit, passive, and listen
to the treadmill requiems of the old Church
somehow expressing the life of my father
as the love of a man who believed his American
Dream, seeing cities and fruit on the plains
enough for everyone and a decent wage for
every worker (as long as he's white)
happy children and pride in himself

ETERNAL REST GRANT UNTO THEM O
LORD and LET PERPETUAL LIGHT SHINE
UPON THEM
                    after the gospel on Lazarus
I stood and read:
    For our brother, Arthur, that he
    who knew both joy and suffering
    here may share Christ's pasch
    new life and happiness
    let us pray to the Lord.
and how indeed both joy and suffering from him
he was a good man but was possessed

That afternoon we went over to Miramar
Naval Air Station   biggest in the world
and we rode down avenues of napalm pods
bombs and rockets and O Jesus!
billions for death, hooray!
the jets practice takeoff and landing
my brother-in-law said
this one pilot out of control bailed out
the plane slammed into a hangar
19 guys were killed in that one, two of
my best buddies he said in his Georgia way

and he showed us the golf courses swimming
pools tennis courts the Navy pays off its own
the decent wage of the American Dream

and the mothball fleet we saw that too
their destroyer cannon capped the quad 40s
covered with upside down bowls
gray gray fleet still in the harbors of war
so that when hours passed the moonlight
so white shone a ghastly plain on San Diego
I thought of what my brother had said when I
asked him didn't he think the generals had
got too much power
                    if they'd a listened
5 years ago he said all this mess would be over
go in and wipe 'em out
I wanted to tell him what the Leicester students
were told by a gas station attendant
I do approve the guy said of killing them
students   I think they oughta have a quota
bag so many protesters a day
N.Y. hard hat workers beating up people

I didn't say anything   I somehow knew
what he was thinking   he was thinking
we are the most powerful country in
the world and the only force for good
and we will do as we damn well please
and if you try to stop us killing gook
communists we'll turn on you too

I flew out of San Diego and I said Cynthia
God I been in the heart of the military-
industrial complex I been in the home of
the silent majority they have a concrete pool
a concrete lawn plastic flowers and spend their
time worrying about if their fences are
high enough to wall out the strangers nearby

and Phil was with the kids and Cynthia to pick
my bewildered self up at Logan
we hugged and talked (him telling about some
lady Swami Rosenbloom in the Poconos how
she was supposed to have this ashram a
spiritual creature vegetarian hindoo
stuffing hamburgs down her little boy's
throat—eat! eat!)
him getting ready to go across America
Oregon farm land and live in a commune
and teach yoga
                         as he did that night with us
exercise rituals to the sun-god
and Phil spoke of stilling the mind

Phil spent the night there in the Trappist
monastery in Spencer   meditating
and when we went to see him
he said he spent his day in the woods
saw a garter snake some ducks a cracked monk
heard bells
                         then Friday the 22nd we took him
up to what we thought was the Leyden commune
only to discover it had moved was called
THE BROTHERHOOD OF THE SPIRIT
it was evening we talked in the dark with Nate
and David while Benny (who is shy)
just came sailing into the place so easy
playing in a dirtpile he called his volcano
singing his song VOLCANO VOLCANO VIA FEE!
Billy into the treehouse   Cynthia in talisman talk
to a girl named Robin

I don't know what to do next I said
the country's coming apart   everything is breaking
teaching the regular way doesn't seem enough
I just want to sit and talk with people about books
writing papers and all that doesn't make it

some part of me is dead to all that now

they eased me
you can find the strength to free yourself
to be happy they said
just look for the spirit in you   in every man
and find a way to love that
speech to that god within everyone is joy
and perfect understanding
help others to get beyond the illusion
of their hangups   that is not the essential
you   God is the essential   love THAT

we had to give up the world in order
to be free to give ourselves to the world

when I spoke of Plato and Emerson they
smiled and wanted me to know they lived
the texts

I said I've got to find a way to make a break
come and live with us they said
WE HAVE WHAT YOU ARE LOOKING FOR
O God, if only I could find the courage
you have the courage just let it be
stay with us and listen to our words
right now I hope someone has shanghaied
your wife and talking her into staying
I felt a fear she nightly would find some
one she would love better than me
Cynthia said all we know is that Bill is a poet
he's a MAN said David A MAN FIRST

and the place was lit by psychic lanterns
and love, love it ruled the stars

at Jim and Chris's place in Amherst
I got drunk telling of the BROTHERHOOD

which allows no booze   could I be free of booze?
I read Chris's palm and saw a line cutting
through the marriage M and said if anyone has
reservations about this marriage it's you
and this hurt Jim and I was hurt too
and I wondered if I would be such a stupid ass
at the SPIRIT and I figured I would
this evil in us   this imp of the perverse
is no illusion I thought there's something too
simplistic in their philosophy

we went there again the next day
but the vibes weren't as good and we left feeling
we'd have to work out our own commune
we talked to Phil   I'm gone already he said
to fulfill my dream, my voyage in search of
my soul and I'll be going west because Diane
is taking Arieh to California and I want to be
near him
              he didn't know but what he might
search the whole world over and find that
THE BROTHERHOOD OF THE SPIRIT was
the community and come back.

I copied down from the wall, this:

SPIRITUAL LAW

I am spirit
I am vibrating
creative energy.

I vow to do
obey, and be
the will of
creative energy.

I vow to loose

myself from my
carnal self.
So be it.

When I showed it to Jim he said
they don't give the body it's due
there's too much emphasis on the spirit
they lack ambiguity   paradox
I hugged him and said I love you
I like you too he said   we laughed
and always between us there's the question
have you written anything lately?
and I have not been about to write till now
do you see why now, Jim?

riding back to Leicester from Amherst
Cynthia and I talked about the idea of moving out
of the big house   making a commune of ourselves
living in a tent (if we could borrow one
from Jerry Morgan)

the next day Sunday the 24th of May
we went up to Dick and Beth Chase's
for a guitar and banjo pickin' sing and beer blast
picnic everybody getting high on the music
making new friends
and at nightfall I asked Ellen to write down
the words to song they sang and her husband
Bob did and this is some of what they said:

In a vine-covered shack in the mountains
bravely fighting the battle of time
is that dear one who's weathered those
        sorrows
it's that silver haired Daddy of mine.

and I thought of Arthur Achilles Tremblay
in the sod of El Camino Real
and of Phil already trudging along his way to
his Vermont ashram along his Camino Real
and I knew that more than just my father died
some old self had died in me then and in many
      I saw around me, each in his own time

the time has come
for the living dead in Tijuana, Mexico to kick
the gringos out altogether and be resurrected
for the mothball fleet to dissolve into the pacific
for the stock market to totally crash
      while being hijacked to Cuba

and I'm getting to the point where I don't
      give a shit anymore
about losing my job or being a black sheep
I'm going to write about the spirit I know is
      there in man
and find a way to be happy and loving
and let the old crap of the past go at last
and live free